FROM OUR HEARTS
Shared Family Journal

A Keepsake for the Words
That Bring Your Family Closer

Pat Wyman

From My Heart Publishing

Where we love is home.
Elizabeth Gaskell

Every family story begins not with a plan,
but with being together.

These pages are a place to begin - again and again...

WELCOME TO YOUR FAMILY JOURNAL

Using This Journal

As you open these pages, you'll find something made just for your family. This is a place to savor moments, memories and the small details that make your family uniquely yours.

Over time, these pages become a keepsake shaped by your voices, your laughter, and the life you share together.

From Our Hearts is meant to grow naturally, filled in at your own pace, in your own way.

This journal belongs to everyone in your family. There's no right way to use it and no need to do everything at once. Write, draw, add notes, or include anything else that feels meaningful.

Initial your entries if you'd like, so you remember who shared what. Keep it light. Enjoy the moments. Let your family's story unfold one page at a time.

Inside These Pages...

These pages reflect what your life actually looks like...the regular days, the small moments and the in-between stuff that makes it yours, right here, right now.

These pages hold your family's current favorites – the songs on repeat, comfort watches and things everyone keeps talking about. Someday, flipping back through the time capsules will be a fun reminder of what filled your home during this season of life.

Every family has superpowers. Not the flying-through-the-air kind, but the real-life kind that keep things moving, lighten the mood, and help you handle whatever comes up.

These pages are for the fun side of being a family...the inside jokes, moments that make sense only to you, the made-up traditions, and the kind of laughter that makes everyone happy to be part of your family.

These pages give your family a place to notice the good you bring to one another, turning everyday appreciation into moments that feel warm, genuine and easy to say out loud, even when life is busy.

Some things are memorable because they're meaningful. Others are memorable because they're just funny, and they stick around in your family. These pages are for the fond memories that make up your everyday life and you'll enjoy looking at them in the future...

This last page is here to help you mark the end of your shared journal experience in a simple, meaningful way.

SECTION 1

Right Here...Right Now

These pages reflect what our life
actually looks like...the regular days,
the small moments and the in-between stuff
that makes it ours, right here, right now.

OUR FAMILY PHOTO.
RIGHT HERE. RIGHT NOW.

Names: _______________________________ Date: _______________

____

____

If our family were a soundtrack, what would it sound like? Would it be one steady song, or all about different styles? What makes the sound feel like *us*?

Here's one way
a family answered...

Our soundtrack sounds like a mix. Music, voices, and running commentary happening at once. Another said it sounded like a TV show theme. It's familiar, lively, and instantly recognizable as theirs.

If someone walked through our door right now, what would be the very first clue that this family has a personality of its own?

One family said:

Probably the half-finished craft project on the table, how shoes and coats are everywhere, and the way everyone talks at once, but we somehow understand each other.

What is one small silly thing in our family that serves absolutely no purpose, except that we love laughing about it?

We keep opening and closing the fridge, even when we already know what's inside. It's as if we're convinced something new might magically appear.

What little family quirk makes perfect sense to us but would probably confuse anyone else?

> We often speak like sports announcers to each other from across the room. Nobody asked us to. It just happens and we love it.

What do we do as a family that feels totally normal to us, but if someone filmed it, it would probably make us laugh?

Whenever one person cannot find their phone, two people are calling it, and one person is already holding a flashlight, finding it in the exact place that was already checked.

What is something we hope never changes about our family rhythm?

How we check
in with each other
with a simple
"You good?" that
somehow says
everything.

If our home could speak, which spot would spill the most secrets about who we are?

> The wall of photos that tracks every haircut, every birthday, and every goofy phase we lived through.

What amusing thing happened this week that our family somehow never quite finished or followed through on?

We always say, "Let's repair that in a second," until we discovered that "a second" is not a real unit of time in our family.

Who ended up at the center of today's story, and what made them shine?

Someone shared a win, and the whole family cheered like it was national news.

If we could tweak one tiny thing to make life smoother for all of us, which one would we happily agree on together?

Maybe deciding what to eat before everyone gets hungry and all logic disappears.

Family Artwork

Drawings, doodles or sketches that inspire us.

Notes

Thoughts about this section we want to remember.

SECTION 2

Family Time Capsules

These pages are for our current favorites...
the songs on repeat, comfort watches and things
we can't stop talking about. Later, they'll be a fun
reminder of what was popular around here.

FAMILY TIME CAPSULE

Music on Repeat

Date: _______________________

The song and artist I can't stop playing right now.

Initials

_______________________________________ _________

_______________________________________ _________

_______________________________________ _________

_______________________________________ _________

_______________________________________ _________

_______________________________________ _________

_______________________________________ _________

FAMILY TIME CAPSULE

Comfort Watch

Date: ______________________________

The show or movie I keep going back to lately:

Initials

FAMILY TIME CAPSULE

My "Favorite Place" Right Now:

Date: _______________________

Where I feel happiest lately...real or imaginary:

Initials

FAMILY TIME CAPSULE

Current Interest

Date: ________________________

What I'm really into right now...hobby, sport, trend, etc.

Initials

FAMILY TIME CAPSULE

Treat of the Moment

Date: _______________________________

The snack/food/drink I'm always craving lately:

Initials

FAMILY TIME CAPSULE

People I am Spending Time With...

Date: _______________________

People I've been hanging out with the most lately:

Initials

____ ___________

____ ___________

____ ___________

____ ___________

____ ___________

____ ___________

____ ___________

____ ___________

FAMILY TIME CAPSULE

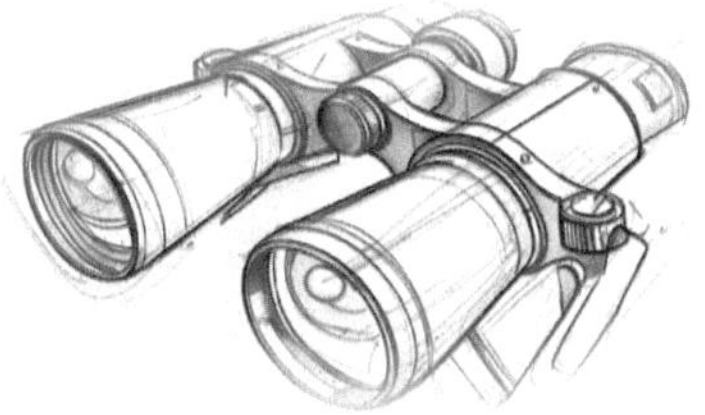

Looking Ahead

Date: ________________________

Something I'm excited about in the next few months:

Initials

FAMILY TIME CAPSULE

One thing that feels like progress right now…

Date: _______________________

Anything that feels like a step forward...

Initials

FAMILY TIME CAPSULE

A parent's or guardian's family time capsule.

Date: _________________________

What I want to remember about our family this season:

Initials

FAMILY TIME CAPSULE

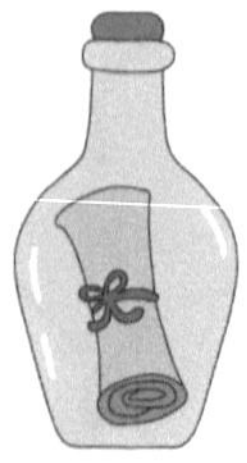

One message I want to share with my family today to read years from now:

Date: _______________________

A thought, a wish or something you want us to remember.

Initials

____ ___________

____ ___________

____ ___________

____ ___________

____ ___________

____ ___________

____ ___________

____ ___________

Family Artwork

Sketches or drawings of any time capsules we love...

Notes

Thoughts about this section we want to remember.

SECTION 3

Our Family's Superpowers

Every family has superpowers.

Not the flying-through-the-air kind, the real-life kind
that keep things moving, lighten the mood, and help
you handle whatever comes up.

If our family were a superhero team, what would we be called and what would our team's superpower be?

Our team is called "One More Minute" Group. Our superpower is stretching time just a little.

What is something each person in our family brings that makes us stronger together?

> Everyone contributes
> something different.
> One brings humor,
> one brings calm,
> one brings snacks,
> and somehow it all
> balances out. (Names
> and superpower listed
> below)

When something unexpected happens, what is our family's automatic response as a team?

Our superpower is all-hands-on-deck energy. One thing goes awry and suddenly everyone is involved… snacks appear, tasks get claimed, and things start moving.

What does everyone in our family somehow have superpower knowledge about at the same time?

Whatever is happening right now. Suddenly everyone has instant expertise.

What usually makes our family laugh when the moment needs it?

Someone exaggerates what's happening, says the quiet part out loud or repeats a familiar line, and suddenly everyone's laughing.

What does our family do better together than any of us could do alone?

Our superpower is teamwork without overthinking it. Everyone takes a small piece of a large task, and somehow it all comes together.

When plans change at the last minute, what's our family superpower move?

We complain briefly, regroup quickly, and somehow act as if the new plan was the idea all along.

What would our family be famous for if anyone were watching?

{ We all love standing around together deciding what to do next... }

What does our family feel confident about...even without proof?

That everything will work out. No plan, no proof, just confidence.

What does our family instantly generate more of than anyone asked for?

> Our "more of" superpower… opinions. No matter the topic, everyone has one within seconds.

Family Artwork

**Draw your family as a superhero team.
Imagination encouraged.** 😊

Notes

Use this space for extra superpowers, inside jokes, quiet strengths, or last-minute ideas. Future-you will be very glad you wrote these down.

SECTION 4
Playful Pages

These pages are for the fun side of being a family...
the inside jokes, moments that make sense only to
you, the made-up traditions, and the kind of laughter
that makes everyone happy to be part of our family.

What moment still makes our family laugh long after it happened?

> The great spaghetti disaster of last year! We are still laughing about it.

What is our family's funniest 'only in this house' phrase or expression?

We say this and only our family knows the backstory: How much wood would a woodchuck chuck if a woodchuck could chuck wood?

What could be one new and fun family tradition we start?

> We would take an annual blurry photo of everyone with the caption: We absolutely had a plan but...

What harmless family habit would be weird in public but totally normal at home?

> We have full conversations through exaggerated facial expressions across the room like we're in a silent movie.

What game (real or invented) does our family always end up playing when we have time together?

We made up a game with rules so complicated that even we forget them. It involves touch football, playing offense and defense at the same time…

People who love to eat are always the best people.
Julia Child

What debate or food-related moment in our family is secretly comedy gold?

We can turn a simple question like "What's for dinner?" into a 20-minute debate with strong opinions and no solution.

If our family were accidentally photographed for a magazine, what would the caption say?

Family realizing an important point is being made but no one remembers what it was anymore.

What is the funniest thing our family does when we're all in a good mood?

We turn the kitchen into a tiny concert venue, complete with dance moves that should never be recorded.

What completely ordinary family moment somehow turns into chaos every single time?

Trying to leave
the house "on time."
It starts calm, then
shoes disappear,
someone suddenly
needs the bathroom,
and at least one
person announces
they're starving.

What small, silly detail about our family makes us smile every time?

> We all freeze dramatically whenever someone drops something, like it's a major event, and then immediately go back to normal like it never happened.

Family Artwork

Your place to sketch or draw your family
doing anything that makes you laugh.

Notes

Use this space for extra jokes, funny quotes someone said, new traditions you invent, or anything that didn't fit on the pages above. Your future you will love this.

SECTION 5

Gratitude Pages

These pages give your family a place to notice the good you bring to one another, turning everyday appreciation into moments that feel warm, genuine and easy to say out loud, even when life is busy.

What is one thing we truly appreciate about each person in our family?

For these pages, place the name of one family member at the top. Everyone else adds one thing they appreciate about that person and signs their initials.

Name: _______________________________

Initials

Name: ___________________________

Initials

♡ ____ ___________

♡ ____ ___________

♡ ____ ___________

♡ ____ ___________

♡ ____ ___________

♡ ____ ___________

♡ ____ ___________

♡ ____ ___________

Name: ___________________________

Initials

♡ ____ ___________

♡ ____ ___________

♡ ____ ___________

♡ ____ ___________

♡ ____ ___________

♡ ____ ___________

♡ ____ ___________

♡ ____ ___________

Name: _______________________________

Initials

$\heartsuit$ ____ _________

$\heartsuit$ ____ _________

$\heartsuit$ ____ _________

$\heartsuit$ ____ _________

$\heartsuit$ ____ _________

$\heartsuit$ ____ _________

$\heartsuit$ ____ _________

$\heartsuit$ ____ _________

Name: _______________________________

Initials

$\heartsuit$ ____ _________

$\heartsuit$ ____ _________

$\heartsuit$ ____ _________

$\heartsuit$ ____ _________

$\heartsuit$ ____ _________

$\heartsuit$ ____ _________

$\heartsuit$ ____ _________

$\heartsuit$ ____ _________

Name: ___________________________________

Initials

♡ ____   ________

♡ ____   ________

♡ ____   ________

♡ ____   ________

♡ ____   ________

♡ ____   ________

♡ ____   ________

♡ ____   ________

Name: ___________________________________

Initials

♡ ____   ________

♡ ____   ________

♡ ____   ________

♡ ____   ________

♡ ____   ________

♡ ____   ________

♡ ____   ________

♡ ____   ________

What is something ordinary in our family life that we're quietly grateful for right now?

What is something about being together as a family that we appreciate more these days?

What is something about our home or routine that makes everyday life feel good here?

Family Artwork

Notes

Space for extra thoughts, additional thank-yous,
and things you want to remember later.

Fun Things We Might Want to Write Down

Some things are memorable because they're meaningful. Others are memorable because they're just funny, and they stick around in our family. These pages are for the fond memories that make up our everyday lives...

Phrases that pop up all the time in our family...

Rules we all know and regularly ignore, like not feeding the dog from the table... 😃

Things that always seem to disappear in our house no matter how much we look for them...

Things our family always comments on...

Things that tend to always end up on the counter but we're not sure why...

Things we tend to do during a favorite time of year...

Plans that tend to change halfway through...

Things in the house that get "moved for now" but usually stay there forever...

Family Artwork

Anything that inspires you...

Notes

Just one more page to go...

SECTION 7

As Our Family Finishes This Journal

Final Thoughts...

As we completed our journal, what did we notice or discover along the way that we didn't expect?

When we look back on this journal, what do we want to remember most?

Tell Us About Your Experience.

If this journal created meaningful conversations, laughter, and special moments for your family, we would be grateful if you would take one minute to share your experience.

https://forms.gle/WHDA3yz35MLZbMwf9

Scan here to share your experience.
Responses are anonymous and emails are not collected.

Thank you. Your feedback helps this journal reach more families.

Keep the Connection Going!

There is a gift for your family on the next page.

A Thank-You Gift for Your Family

A beautifully designed set of pages that keeps the talking, laughing,
and connection going even after the journal is finished.
Scan the QR code to receive your PDF.

https://www.FromMyHeartPublishing.com/remember

A Note About the Family Connection Initiative

The Family Connection Initiative exists to create meaningful offline experiences that help families stay personally connected in an increasingly digital world.

Through journals and thoughtful shared projects, the initiative invites families to step away from screens for a bit, slow down, and reconnect in ways that feel real, present, and lasting.

About the Author

Pat Wyman is a best-selling author, founder of the Family Connection Initiative and HowtoLearn.com, a trusted learning resource that has supported families and teachers for decades. Her work has been shared in schools and homes worldwide, guided by one simple belief: when families feel connected, people are happier and life feels easier.

That belief is deeply personal. Because her father served in the military, Pat's family moved often, and home felt temporary. Losing her father at twelve and her mother in her early thirties shaped her understanding of how deeply presence, continuity, and connection matter.

Wanting others to feel supported and confident, Pat became a teacher and learning expert. She saw that when learning challenges ease, confidence grows and relationships strengthen making learning as much about feeling valued as academics.

That insight shaped her writing. As daily life grows busier and more screen-centered, Pat creates experiences that feel personal and lasting. Her work has earned the trust of families and corporations, including a Microsoft-sponsored book. Her first journal, *The One-Minute Gratitude Journal for the Moments That Matter*, grew into the Family Connection Initiative, a series designed to strengthen relationships through reflection, laughter, and gratitude, while creating lasting keepsakes.

If your family enjoyed this journal, a short review on Amazon helps it reach more families.

ISBN: 978-1-890047-30-6 * First Edition * Printed in the United States of America. For permissions and requests contact FromMyHeartPublishing.com * OurHeartsConnect@gmail.com

Special Editions & Community Distribution.

This book is available for sponsored distribution through organizations, companies and community partners committed to strengthening family relationships in a screen-filled world.

Customized editions may include: Personalized or branded messages; bulk distribution for families, schools, military communities, or employees; community wellness and connection initiatives. To explore sponsoring this book for families in your community or organization, please contact: OurHeartsConnect@gmail.com.

More Journals by Pat Wyman

https://amzn.to/487SKLB

A guided journal designed to help you pause, reflect, and appreciate the good in your life.

With just one minute a day, you can build a powerful habit of gratitude that brings more positivity into your life each day.

www.ingramcontent.com/pod-product-compliance
Lightning Source LLC
Chambersburg PA
CBHW031353060726
47590CB00007B/2762